T0207623

My
Sanctuary,
A Spiritual Journal

JEWEL HARPER

WESTBOW
PRESS®
A DIVISION OF THOMAS NELSON
& ZONDERVAN

Copyright © 2011, 2015 Jewel Harper-Simon.

Author Credits: Footsteps to Christ

All rights reserved. No part of this book may be used or reproduced by any means, graphic, electronic, or mechanical, including photocopying, recording, taping or by any information storage retrieval system without the written permission of the publisher except in the case of brief quotations embodied in critical articles and reviews.

The views expressed in this work are solely those of the author and do not necessarily reflect the views of the publisher, and the publisher hereby disclaims any responsibility for them.

Excerpts are adapted and compiled by Jewel Harper.

All rights reserved. No part of this book may be reproduced in any form without permission in writing from the publishers.

Scripture taken from The Message. Copyright © 1993, 1994, 1995, 1996, 2000, 2001, 2002. Used by permission of NavPress Publishing Group.

The excerpt from Alcoholics Anonymous and the Twelve Steps have been adapted and reprinted. With the following inserts:

The Twelve Steps does not mean that AAWS has reviewed or approved the contents of this publication, or that AAWS necessarily agrees with the views expressed herein. AA is a program of recovery from alcoholism only. While AA is a spiritual program, it is not a religious program. AA is not affiliated or allied with any sect, denomination, or specific religious belief.

WestBow Press books may be ordered through booksellers or by contacting:

WestBow Press
A Division of Thomas Nelson & Zondervan
1663 Liberty Drive
Bloomington, IN 47403
www.westbowpress.com
1 (866) 928-1240

Because of the dynamic nature of the Internet, any web addresses or links contained in this book may have changed since publication and may no longer be valid. The views expressed in this work are solely those of the author and do not necessarily reflect the views of the publisher, and the publisher hereby disclaims any responsibility for them.

Any people depicted in stock imagery provided by Thinkstock are models, and such images are being used for illustrative purposes only. Certain stock imagery © Thinkstock.

ISBN: 978-1-5127-0619-2 (sc)
ISBN: 978-1-5127-0620-8 (hc)
ISBN: 978-1-5127-0618-5 (e)

Library of Congress Control Number: 2015912421

Print information available on the last page.

WestBow Press rev. date: 12/31/2015

CONTENTS

INTRODUCTION

My Sanctuary is a personal guide to understanding the twelve-step program of long-term recovery and how it can be integrated biblically with a Christian perspective. I believe that Scripture and the twelve steps are both important healing tools that you can apply to your lives; you can open yourselves to God's grace, mercy, and unconditional love. The main theme of *My Sanctuary* is that healing is possible. Everyone can experience a sanctuary where wounds can heal.

Why a spiritual recovery journal? It is a record of your addiction and those experiences and thoughts you deem valuable. Within the workbook you will be able to preserve those interactions, events, and reflections that trace your personal history with God. This material is for mature adults who have experienced feelings of guilt and shame; low self-esteem; low self-worth; anxiety; and unworthiness. It is also for those who have been hiding their addictions and are fearful of sharing and surrendering them. This journal will help you replace those behaviors with spiritual strength.

This journal will be an awakening to God's compassion and His grace. The twelve steps and accompanying Scripture passages help you rediscover and deepen your spiritual life and develop a personal transformation. This book provides an opportunity for you to develop balance and establish a renewed relationship with God.

My Sanctuary: A Spiritual Journal brings a voice and message that combine to project the sense of a seasoned mentor accompanying the reader on a journey. Rather than giving a blank journal to someone working through the twelve steps of recovery, the book offers guidance, rhythm, routine, and a common approach to reflecting upon the spiritual dimensions of recovery. One can gain a sense of this approach by reading the following passage from Step Seven:

> Step Seven conveys an important part of the cleansing process and prepares me for the next stage of my journey. I need to get out of the way so that God can do His work in me. I humbly ask for the removal of my shortcomings and give God complete control to work in my life. While working on the first six steps, I became aware of my problems. I looked at my life with honesty and saw hidden aspects of myself. Now I have a realistic view of myself and my place in the world. I became ready for God to change my attitudes and behaviors. Step Seven presents me with the opportunity to turn to God and ask for removal of those parts of my character that cause pain, including character defects, my faulty belief systems, and unhealthy patterns of behavior. In Step Seven, humility means understanding my role in my life's journey,

appreciating my strengths and limitations, and having faith in God.

One of the strengths of this book is the opportunity it provides for the reader to interact with the content by reflecting upon and recording answers to the questions.

In memory of Lena Keesee-Harper, family, friends, and others who have struggled with addiction, and to those who have not yet discovered that a sanctuary is a place that leads to long-term recovery.

My Sanctuary

My Sanctuary is a place of peace and of new beginnings.

No more battles about my past,

No more wrestling matches about my addictions.

Removing my mask, no dishonesty and denial.

My Sanctuary

Is a place to understand myself and surrender my life—

Learning about my God,

Growing in spirituality, and developing
my personal transformation.

My Sanctuary

Is a place where I go for comfort when I need
support and encouragement—God is there.

I can trust and surrender.

When my pain and hurts are so overwhelming,
I cry out "Thy will be done!"

I learn how to pray and meditate;

I study the word of God.

I learn about Jesus Christ, my Lord and Savior.

My Sanctuary

Is where I have learned what serenity means.

I learned about humility.

My faith, it grows

In my Sanctuary.

—Rev. Jewel Harper, MPA, MDiv

STEP ONE

You admitted you are powerless over your addiction
and that your life had become unmanageable.

In your life, God is all-powerful. He is perfect, and He gives you the freedom to make choices. He wants you to make something of your life, but you know you are powerless and need His intervention and help in your life every day.

In Step One, you have come to realize the truth about addictions: they will take total control over your life—physically, mentally, and spiritually. Recovery means first admitting defeat and recognizing that your addiction has the power in your life and is an obsessive trait. That obsessive trait has produced unhealthy behaviors that come to light in the way you try to manage your life. You are mired in an addictive process that has rendered you powerless over your behavior. You can no longer manage or control your life. In your abstinence, recovery will begin. Learning to apply the spiritual principles of being honest, open, and willing will help you begin to heal.

You are able to apply Step One in your life-journey by being *open* to looking at areas in your life in which you have been in denial. You can do this by becoming totally *honest*—dropping the mask—seeing things the way they really are in your life, and looking at how some parts of your life have been impaired, abnormal, and dysfunctional because of your addiction. Changes will occur as you work the steps. Your *willingness* to work the steps will enable you to begin healing, to have a spiritual awakening to God's purpose and plan in your life, and to help others. Now you can say, "In working Step One, I have now accepted my addiction."

Step One Study Guide

If the power of sin within me keeps sabotaging my best intentions,
I obviously need help! I realize that I don't have what it takes. I can
will it, but I can't do it. I decide to do good, but I don't really do it;
I decide not to do bad, but then I do it anyway. My decisions, such
as they are, don't result in actions. Something has gone wrong deep
within me and gets the better of me every time. (Romans 7:18–20)

I'm tired of all this—so tired. I am worn out from crying. My bed
has been floating forty days and nights. (Psalm 6:6–7)

What pain are you experiencing at this time in your life?

_____

_____

_____

_____

_____

_____

_____

How have you lost self-respect due to your addiction? Include a
description of your behavior and feelings.

_____

_____

_____

_____

_____

_____

_____

What is it about your behavior that your spouse, partner or companion, family, and friends object to most? Identify some of your weaknesses.

_____

_____

_____

_____

_____

_____

_____

In what areas of your life do you experience the greatest sense of unmanageability? Why don't you trust yourself?

_____

_____

_____

_____

_____

_____

_____

Has your addiction damaged your friendships? What has been the impact?

_____

_____

_____

_____

_____

_____

_____

_____

How has your addiction damaged your employment?

_____

_____

_____

_____

_____

_____

_____

How has it damaged you legally?

_____

_____

_____

_____

_____

_____

_____

How has it damaged you spiritually?

_____

_____

_____

_____

_____

_____

_____

_____

Reflection

_____

_____

_____

_____

_____

_____

_____

_____

_____

_____

_____

_____

_____

_____

_____

_____

_____

_____

_____

_____

_____

_____

_____

_____

_____

_____

_____

_____

_____

_____

_____

_____

_____

Prayer

Lord, today I am accepting my addiction and recognizing the need for help. I feel frightened and unsure of myself. Self-will and denial have kept me from seeing that I have a problem and have become separated from you. I need to be honest and open and to learn more about the disease of addiction. I need to trust and regain my faith in you. I choose today to admit that I am powerless and that my life is unmanageable. Amen.

STEP TWO

> I came to believe that a Power greater than myself
> could restore me to sanity.

As a Christian, you have learned who God is, but you rarely invite His power into your life. Step Two allows you to experience faith and belief as you begin to establish a relationship with God. This relationship provides you with hope, growth, and trust. It becomes an important part of your life. It is here that you develop the foundation for growth in your spiritual life. This growth will help you become the person you want to be. You can begin to take responsibility for your actions. You are no longer acting insane. God is restoring your sanity.

You are able to apply this step to your life as you move toward a long-term recovery program. Wisdom and knowledge are showing you there are only two escapes from addiction: one is insanity; the other is death. Having faith in God is the basic law of recovery. With Step Two, you are able to build a trusting relationship with God. Recovery, therefore, becomes a way of life. Working a long-term recovery program can make all the difference in your life—including your spiritual, physical, and mental well-being; your happiness; and the security of your home and your life. This step will direct you to a mentor, teach you humility, and enable you to grow in love, health, and grace.

Step Two Study Guide

> My grace is enough; it's all you need. My strength
> comes into its own in your weakness. (2 Corinthians
> 12:9)

> Don't panic. I'm with you. There's no need to fear
> for I'm your God. I'll give you strength. I'll help
> you. I'll hold you steady; keep a firm grip on you.
> (Isaiah 41:10)

What activities in your life interfere with your relationship with God?

_____

_____

_____

_____

_____

_____

_____

_____

What are some of your beliefs about God?

_____

_____

_____

_____

_____

_____

_____

_____

What kind of God do you want? What does He expect of you? What do you expect of Him?

_____

_____

_____

_____

_____

_____

_____

_____

Reflection

_____

_____

_____

_____

_____

_____

_____

_____

_____

_____

_____

_____

_____

_____

_____

_____

_____

_____

_____

_____

_____

_____

_____

Prayer

To you, my Lord and Savior, I pray for my mind to be clear and open to hear your wisdom in understanding addiction. Teach me to trust you and to believe in you. I pray for honesty, an open mind, and increased faith. Lord, I don't want to be without you again. Amen.

STEP THREE

I made a decision to turn my will and my life over
to the care of God as I understood Him.

Step Three calls for a decision. In Step Three, you are putting your belief about God into action. You are willing, at this point, to allow God to work in your life. This decision requires that you move away from your self-will. Self-will is composed of character defects, such as closed-mindedness, unwillingness, self-centeredness, and outright defiance. Your self-centered obsession will keep you trapped in a continuous cycle of fear and pain. But because you believe that there is growth in taking action despite your fear or uncertainty, you are able to trust that your life will change. It will take determination, time, and courage for you to change. Step Three is your commitment to your own emotional, physical, and spiritual well-being. You can now learn how to stop struggling by letting go and trusting God.

Step Three can be applied to your long-term recovery journey. As you surrender your life and stop carrying the burdens of your past, you will begin to feel better about yourself. You will turn away from behaviors that foster addiction, discouragement, sickness, and fear. The more you learn to trust God, the more you will extend that trust to others. The decision to choose God's way will restore you to the fullness of life. As you become free from self-will, you will in turn free yourself from many negative behaviors, and you will be able to deal more effectively with the daily routine of your life. As you come to know God's love, you will yearn to share it with others. God offers you a life that is free from the emotional pollution of your past. Choosing this life allows you to enjoy new and wonderful experiences. Your life will transform into a dynamic relationship with God.

As you find a personal understanding of Step Three and how it will work in your life-journey, you will continue your efforts to develop a personal relationship with God. You are also able to give up your efforts to control everything around you. You now are able to release the burdens you have been carrying and turn them over to God's care. You are now able to shift your focus away from your own self-interest toward a more spiritually centered life. With guidance from a sponsor, spiritual mentor, or an accountability group, you will be able to apply spiritual principles and biblical growth to shift your focus away from your own self-interest and toward a life of humility that is spiritually centered.

Step Three Study Guide

> Are you tired? Worn out? Burned out on religion?
> Come to me. Get away with me and you'll recover
> your life. I'll show you how to take a real rest. Walk
> with me and work with me—watch how I do it.
> Learn the unforced rhythms of grace. I won't lay
> anything heavy or ill-fitting on you. Keep company
> with me and you'll learn to live freely and lightly.
> (Matthew 11:28–30)

Which parts of your life are you unwilling to turn over to God? Explain why.

_____

_____

_____

_____

_____

_____

_____

_____

List a few worries, fears, or resentments that are troubling you.

_____

_____

_____

_____

_____

_____

_____

_____

Are you willing to surrender them to God's care? If not, why?

_____

_____

_____

_____

_____

_____

_____

_____

(We must surrender or turn over those behaviors that foster addiction, discouragement, sickness, and fear.)

Reflection

_____

_____

_____

_____

_____

_____

_____

_____

_____

Prayer

God, daily I offer myself to you, asking you to build me up, so that your will be done in me. Relieve me of the bondage of self-will and the need to control so I may better do your will. Take away my battles, problems, and struggles so that victory over them may be a witness to those I will help. May I be a servant to you and do your will always. Amen.

STEP FOUR

I made a searching and fearless moral inventory of
myself.

In Step Four, you realize certain areas of your life need attention.
You also realize that you cannot see all of those areas. Taking a
moral inventory will expose the harmful character traits of your
addicted personality. The gravity of your addiction problems is deep-
seated; it involves self-centered habits, physical health, emotions, and
misconceptions acquired over a period of years. A moral inventory
of a lifetime of addiction is not quickly recorded, nor is it a record
that can be simply stated. It must be honest, sincere, and thorough.
Addictions have sapped your mental powers, weakened your physical
resistance, and sponsored irrational thought and action. This has
caused you extreme mental and physical hardship and has brought
anxiety and suffering to others. Denial has kept you blinded for
years to the dirt in the corners of your life. Low self-esteem has
kept you ignorant of the beauty and worth of your life. In this step,
God comes to you as a caring friend. God opens your eyes to the

weaknesses in your life that need changing and helps you to build on your strengths.

As a Christian believer, your life is one of long-term recovery, spiritual growth, and personal transformation—open-minded to guidance, direction, and change as a person. As you have matured as a believer, the Bible asked you to examine yourself. You are realizing that you wear a mask: one that smiles and lies and hides your feelings. You now realize it is important to take off the mask that you have been wearing since you were a child. You began to remove your mask, and your self-deception began to diminish. You can begin to identify your multiple addictions. You can now take a moral inventory. In Step Four, you continue to embark on a search for insight into self, your feelings, your fears, your resentments, and the patterns of behavior that make up your life. Step Four is a turning point in your life-journey. It is a time for deep personal reflection. It is time for you to develop a sponsor/and or spiritual mentor that will keep you focused on spirituality, humility, honesty, listening, and a willingness to change.

Step Four Study Guide

> Let's take a good look at the way we're living and
> reorder our lives under God. (Lamentations 3:40)

Create a prayer that God will provide insight regarding your
weakness and that He will help you have a healthier life as you work
through your moral inventory.

_____

_____

_____

_____

_____

_____

_____

_____

Resentments

Who are you angry and bitter with?	Why?	What is your part? What could you have done?

People you harmed

List Who you have harmed?	Why?	What could you have done?

Fears

What are your fears?	Why?	What can you do?

Sexual Conduct

List Incest, prostitution, abortions, and pornography (please include online sexual conduct)	Why?	What is your part? What could you have done?

List Painful and Hurtful Experiences

List painful experiences that has been done to you	Why?	What could you have done?

Reflection

Which past failure/hurt causes you to be sad?

_____

_____

_____

_____

_____

_____

_____

_____

_____

_____

_____

_____

_____

_____

_____

_____

_____

_____

_____

_____

_____

_____

Prayer

Dear Lord, today I will begin the process of examining myself and review how I made my life a mess. Remove my fears, worries, and anger. I realize by viewing the list of people I have harmed, I cannot undo it, but I can learn from my past. My choices and mistakes are mine, and I will begin my moral inventory by writing and identifying my wrongs. I pray for the strength to complete the task.

STEP FIVE

I admitted to God, to myself, and to other human beings the exact nature of my wrongs.

Step Five is about spiritual principles, such as surrender, honesty, trust, faith, willingness, and courage. As you work on Step Five, you make an affirmation of commitment to long-term recovery. You admit the exact nature of your wrongs to God, self, and a third person. With Step Five, you surrender the past pains and hurts to another person and begin to feel peace of mind, self-respect, and recovery from addiction. Feelings of shame or fears of change and rejection cannot stop progress; it will only be compounded. Stopping prevents one from moving forward in a long-term recovery. If I stop making every possible effort to recover, I give in to the disease of addiction or death.

Facing and overcoming fear require significant lifestyle changes. Working Step Five with courage shows trust and helps reestablish a relationship with God. Step Five is done with a person of confidence that understands recovery. For this reason, a member of the clergy, a psychiatrist, counselor, sponsor, or doctor is recommended.

I have found that there are areas in my life that need attention. I have come to realize that I cannot see all those areas. I am able to see unconditional love and feel acceptance and belonging from the person with whom I share my confession. Taking an inventory is a lifelong process. God gives us a promise in his word about confession. He tells us that when we confess our sins he will forgive us and cleanse us from our wrongs. Here in Step Five we can learn a lot about humility, hope, and peace. We can now look at our own character defects, admit our wrongs, and ask for forgiveness. Forgiveness is an area that you often fail to look at, though God has given it to us as a gift. We will also be able to learn about forgiveness and letting go when we confess. Forgiveness can be a difficult challenge, but it's even more stressful to hold on to resentments. There are several symbolic letting-go rituals that help with the process. If we have trouble forgiving someone else, we write a letter expressing all of our feelings and explaining why you need to let go. You do not mail that letter—it is cathartic just to write it all down. You write down all of your excess "baggage" on a piece of paper and burn it or cast it into the sea in a bottle when you are ready to really let go.

Step Five Study Guide

> Make this your common practice: Confess your sins
> to each other and pray for each other so that you can
> live together whole and healed. (James 5:16)

> If we confess our sins, he is faithful and just and
> will forgive us our sins and purify us from all
> unrighteousness. (1 John 1:9)

Describe your feelings while making your personal inventory list.

_____

_____

_____

_____

_____

_____

_____

_____

Did you grow closer to God?

_____

_____

_____

_____

_____

_____

_____

_____

In what way has admitting your wrongs helped you to accept my past?

_____

_____

_____

_____

_____

_____

_____

Reflection

_____

_____

_____

_____

_____

_____

_____

_____

_____

_____

_____

_____

_____

_____

_____

_____

_____

_____

_____

_____

_____

Prayer

To you, Lord, who continues to be my great counselor, my life inventory has shown me who I am. It's time for me to admit my wrongs to another person and to you, Lord. Comfort me, and be with me in this step, for without this step I cannot progress in my long-term recovery. With your help, I can do this, and I will do it. Amen.

STEP SIX

I am entirely ready to have God remove all these defects of character.

The spiritual principles of commitment and perseverance help in working Step Six. This is a critical action step. You must take it seriously if you expect to make any significant and lasting changes in your life. Step Six is a process of becoming entirely ready for change. You will strive to increase your readiness throughout your lifetime. You must become entirely ready and open your heart and mind to the deep internal changes that can only be brought about by the presence of your loving God. You are now prepared to surrender your character defects to my loving God.

You are able to apply these principles daily. You must daily surrender your character defects to your loving God because of your attempt to change on your own does not work. You are no longer in denial about or ignorant of your character defects. It hurts us knowing that we have hurt others as a result of our selfishness and self-centeredness. You must begin to find humility. You sense your humanity and realize that you are not perfect. You are able to accept yourself more each day. You can even see more beauty in your life. You must commit daily to your life willingness to change. You see the ongoing battle of fear that results from life stresses, and you see courage and a willingness to face life crises. You must remember that our God, who journey with us and who we are able to surrender our fears to each day, continues to help us persevere we seek a life of harmony and peace. The energy we put into feeding our defects can now be put into nurturing your spiritual goals. The more you focus on your spiritual nature, the more it will unfold in your life. Humility brings us back down to earth and plants your feet on the spiritual path that you are walking. You are learning about tolerance and compassion in action.

Step Six Study Guide

Don't become so well-adjusted to your culture that you fit into it without even thinking. Instead, fix your attention on God. You'll be changed from the inside out. Readily recognize what he wants from you, and quickly respond to it. Unlike the culture around you, always dragging you down to its level of immaturity, God brings the best out of you, develops well-formed maturity in you. (Romans 12:2)

And now bold and free we then become in his presence, freely asking according to his will, sure that he's listening. And if we're confident that he's listening, we know that what we've asked for is as good as ours. (1 John 5:13–15)

So let God work his will in you. Yell a loud no to the Devil and watch him scamper. Say a quiet yes to God and he'll be there in no time. Quit dabbling in sin. Purify your inner life. Quit playing the field. Hit bottom, and cry your eyes out. The fun and games are over. Get serious, really serious. Get down on your knees before the Master; it's the only way you'll get on your feet. (James 4:7–10)

You asked God to remove all character defects that you identified in Steps Four and Five. Write them down and pray for God to remove them. (After ten minutes, destroy the paper.)

_____

_____

_____

_____

_____

_____

_____

_____

Write a letter and thank God. Tell God how you would like to see yourself a year from now!

_____

_____

_____

_____

_____

_____

_____

_____

Reflection

_____

_____

_____

_____

_____

_____

_____

_____

_____

_____

_____

_____

_____

_____

_____

_____

_____

_____

_____

_____

_____

_____

_____

_____

Prayer

Dear God,

I am ready for you to remove from me the character defects that I developed while active in my addiction, which I now realize are obstacles to my long-term recovery. Help me to continue to be honest, to have an open mind, and to be willing to change. Direct and guide me toward a healthy long term recovery lifestyle.

STEP SEVEN

I humbly asked Him to remove all my shortcomings.

Step Seven conveys an important part of the cleansing process and prepares us for the next stage of our journey. You need to get out of the way so that God can do His work in us. You humbly ask for the removal of your shortcomings and give God complete control to work in your life. While working on the first six steps, you became aware of your problems. You looked at your life with honesty and saw hidden aspects of self. Now you have a realistic view of self and your place in the world. You became ready for God to change your attitudes and behaviors. Step Seven presents me with the opportunity to turn to God and ask Him to remove those parts of your character that cause pain, including character defects, your faulty belief systems, and unhealthy patterns of behavior. In Step Seven, humility means understanding my role in my life's journey, appreciating my strengths and limitations, and having faith in God.

You are able to apply Step Seven to your life by progressing toward a happier and healthier life. You see how the opportunities and blessings that God brings into your life surpass anything you could ever have created on your own. You are able to apply this step to your life by letting go of negative behaviors, admitting defeat, recognizing your limitations and asking for help from God. You realize that you are neither more nor less important than anyone else.

Patience is also a part of your life during this step. You understand God's will for us is good and that your faith give us reason to hope for the best. Continuing your relationship with God will go a long way toward increasing your level of comfort while your shortcomings are removed. Continuing to ask God for honesty, open-mindedness, and willingness will help us on our journey through life. With our daily spiritual program, daily prayer, and meditation you are able to glimpse a vision of complete freedom from our shortcomings, knowing that this step is a life process here on earth.

Step Seven Study Guide

> Soak me in your laundry and I'll come out clean,
> scrub me and I'll have a snow-white life. Tune me in
> to foot-tapping songs, set these once-broken bones
> to dancing. Don't look too close for blemishes; give
> me a clean bill of health. God, make a fresh start in
> me, shape a Genesis week from the chaos of my life.
> Don't throw me out with the trash, or fail to breathe
> holiness in me. Bring me back from gray exile, put
> a fresh wind in my sails. (Psalm 51:7–12)

Spend one hour in silence. Pray and meditate and conclude with the Step Seven prayer (below).

Humility implies that I see myself as God sees me. Christ is my example: He emptied Himself to obey God's will, to serve others, and to fulfill God's plan for His life. Can I be Christlike in my humility as I place myself under God's control and submit to His will and plan for my life?

Identify all good memories in your life. If there are none, start by identifying twenty character strengths that you have today.

Identify Good Memories

Jewel Harper

Identify Twenty Character Strengths That You Have Today

Reflection

_____

_____

_____

_____

_____

_____

_____

_____

_____

_____

_____

_____

_____

_____

_____

_____

_____

_____

_____

_____

_____

_____

_____

_____

_____

Prayer

My Creator: I am surrendering myself to you today my weakness and strength. I pray that you remove my weaknesses that stand in the way of my usefulness to you and my brothers and sisters. Give me strength as I go from here to do your good toward those in pain and are hurting that continue to battle the disease of addiction. Amen

STEP EIGHT

I made a list of all persons I had harmed and became
willing to make amends to them all.

Step Eight conveys an awareness of what we have done to others.
Working through the previous steps made it possible to withstand
the pain and remorse of listing the people we have harmed. This
step helps us begin to see beyond the confines of our own life,
and our efforts begin to be more generous. We develop the ability
to feel empathy for others. During Step Eight, we begin to accept
responsibility for our actions, and we do whatever we can to repair
the harm we have done to others. We cause harm when we hurt
someone with our actions. Making amends is accepting the harm
you caused and going to any length to change and avoid repeating
that behavior.

You can apply Step Eight to your life-journey by looking at the
actions that cause you to feel unbearable guilt, shame, and remorse.
We want to be free from guilt by making a list of people we have
harmed, accepting responsibility for the harm we have caused,

learning how to make amends to those you have harmed, and becoming willing to make amends to them. Forgiveness is the key area that you must practice. Your ability to forgive comes from your ability to accept and be compassionate with yourself. You must always pray for whatever it takes to become willing to forgive. Here you learn to accept yourself as you are and to accept others as they are. Here you change your actions and attitudes by understanding how badly you have hurt others, being truly sorry for the pain you have caused, and becoming willing to let them know of your desire to make things right. These are the keys to healing from the past and moving forward.

Step Eight Study Guide

> My dear, dear friends, if God loved us like this, we
> certainly ought to love each other. No one has seen
> God, ever. But if we love one another, God dwells
> deeply within us, and his love becomes complete in
> us—perfect love! (1 John 4:11–12)

> Don't pick on people, jump on their failure, and
> criticize their faults—unless, of course, you want
> the same treatment. Don't condemn those who are
> down; that hardness can boomerang. Be easy on
> people; you'll find life a lot easier. Give away your
> life; you'll find life given back, but not merely given
> back—given back with bonus and blessing. Giving,
> not getting, is the way. Generosity begets generosity.
> (Luke 6:37–38)

Why are you unable to forgive? How is it interfering with your
relationship with God?

_____

_____

_____

_____

_____

_____

_____

_____

Progress and growth in God's kingdom require forgiveness. Why do you suppose this is true in your case?

_____

_____

_____

_____

_____

_____

_____

_____

List of People Harmed	How Harmed	Planned Amends

Reflection

_____

_____

_____

_____

_____

_____

_____

_____

_____

_____

_____

_____

_____

_____

_____

_____

_____

_____

_____

_____

_____

_____

_____

Prayer

Lord: I ask for your help in making a list of all those I have harmed. I will take responsibility for my mistakes and be as forgiving to others as you are forgiving to me. Grant me the willingness to begin my amends. This I pray to my Lord, who did make the greatest sacrifice of forgiveness. Amen.

STEP NINE

I made direct amends to people wherever possible,
except when doing so would injure them or others.

You are making personal or indirect contact with those you have
harmed. Making amends is a two-stage process: making amends to
the person you have harmed, followed up with a behavior change.
God provides you with the wisdom and direction you need to make
amends. Now you must do everything you can to repair the harm
you caused. The spiritual principles of honesty and humility become
invaluable to you in Step Nine. You are able to see how it contributed
to your spiritual growth. Humility is enhanced by your newfound
appreciation of others' feelings.

- improved self-esteem
- capacity to forgive yourself and others
- giving of yourself
- gaining freedom to live in the present (here and now) and
  feelings of belonging in the world.

Your paths is leading you to humility and acceptance acknowledging who you have been and who you are becoming. This behavior change results in a sincere desire to make amends to all those you have harmed. You can't expect your amends to magically heal the hurt feelings of someone you have harmed. You may humbly ask for forgiveness, but if you don't receive it, you let that expectation go, knowing you have done your best. You ask yourself if you are doing this because you are truly sorry and have a genuine desire to make reparations for what you have done. Changing the way you live becomes a lifelong process that includes learning to change your attitude and behavior. Step Nine teaches you a great deal about humility, love, selflessness, and forgiveness.

Step Nine Study Guide

> We, though, are going to love—love and be loved.
> First we were loved, now we love. He loved us first.
> If anyone boasts, "I love God," and goes right on
> hating his brother and sister, thinking nothing of
> it, he is a liar. If he won't love the person he can
> see, how can he love the God he can't see? The
> command we have from Christ is blunt: Loving
> God includes loving people. You've got to love both.
> (1 John 4:19–21)

Who on your amends list causes you the most anxiety?

_____

_____

_____

_____

_____

_____

_____

_____

Describe difficulties you are having in making amends to those who
continue to hold something against you.

_____

_____

_____

_____

_____

_____

_____

_____

Amends should be encouraging and supportive for you and the other person. Are any of your amends not uplifting? Explain.

_____

_____

_____

_____

_____

_____

_____

_____

What rewards (spiritual and emotional) do you expect to receive if you are generous with others?

_____

_____

_____

_____

_____

_____

_____

_____

Write a letter of amends to yourself and then read it while sitting in front of a mirror.

Dear _____,

I was_____(scared, overwhelmed, feeling abandoned, etc.) when _____happened. I forgive myself for the _____(harm done) and anything else I may have done in the past through my thoughts, words, or actions to cause myself harm. I want to make amends to myself about _____. I forgive myself for all the words that I said out of _____ (fear, thoughtlessness, etc.) and confusion.

_____

_____

_____

_____

_____

_____

_____

_____

How do you feel as a result of writing this letter?

_____

_____

_____

_____

_____

_____

_____

_____

Reflection

_____

_____

_____

_____

_____

_____

_____

_____

_____

_____

_____

_____

_____

_____

_____

_____

_____

_____

_____

_____

_____

_____

_____

Prayer

Lord empower me with the right attitude to make my amends, being mindful not to harm others in the process. I ask for your direction and guidance in making indirect amends. I will continue to make amends by working a long-term recovery. Empower me by helping me to abstain from my addictions, helping others, and growing spiritual.

STEP TEN

I continued to take personal inventory and promptly admitted it when I was wrong.

Step Ten is confronting what you have found in yourself. You are able to become more aware of your emotions, your mental state, and your spiritual condition. Step Ten points the way toward continued spiritual growth. It is setting aside time for your personal inventory. A personal inventory is a daily examination of your strengths, weaknesses, motives, and behaviors. It is as important as prayer and Bible study in nurturing your ongoing spiritual growth. Taking daily inventory is not a time-consuming task and can usually be accomplished within fifteen minutes. Step Ten combines all the principles and actions that you are able to apply to your life on a consistent basis. With daily spiritual practice of prayer and meditation and with God's loving presence in your life, you are able to achieve and maintain your newfound balance for the rest of your life.

It is important to monitor yourself for signs of returning to your old attitudes and patterns of behavior. You may be attempting to manage your life alone, manipulating others, or slipping into old patterns of resentment, dishonesty, or selfishness. When you see these temptations arising, you must immediately ask God to forgive you and then make amends where needed. Daily practice of Step Ten maintains honesty and humility and allows you to continue in your development.

You become more conscious of your strengths and weaknesses when you examine your behaviors by taking regular inventory. You are less inclined to yield to feelings of anger, loneliness, and self-righteousness when you are emotionally balanced. Your personal inventory helps you discover who you are, what you are, and where you are going. You might ask questions such as, Were you resentful today? Were you selfish today? Were you dishonest today? Have you kept something to yourself that should be discussed with another person? Were you kind and loving toward others? Could you have done better? Did you think of yourself most? Or were you thinking of others' needs? Did you drift into worry or remorse, which would have diminished your usefulness? After making this review, do you need to ask for God's forgiveness?

Step Ten Study Guide

Everything—and I do mean everything—connected with that old way of life has to go. It's rotten through and through. Get rid of it! And then take on an entirely new way of life—a God-fashioned life, a life renewed from the inside and working itself into your conduct as God accurately reproduces his character in you. (Ephesians 4:22–24)

Have you started to develop and practice good personal habits, such as devotion, exercise, and reading? Using a calendar, such as the one below, plan your good personal habits and make a weekly schedule.

	Sunday	Monday	Tuesday	Wednesday	Thursday	Friday	Saturday
Devotional: Prayer & Meditation							
Readings							
Exercise							
Fellowship Meetings AA/NA Gamblers, Sexual, Overeaters, Shoppers Celebration Recovery Groups							
Bible Study							
Sponsor							
Spiritual Mentor							

Have you asked God to direct your thinking today, especially in areas where you were dishonest and self-pitying?

_____

_____

_____

Were you dishonest today?

_____

_____

_____

Were you resentful today?

_____

_____

_____

Were you selfish today?

_____

_____

_____

Do you owe someone an apology?

_____

_____

_____

Have you kept something to yourself that should be discussed with another person?

_____

_____

_____

Could you have done better?

_____

_____

_____

Did you think of yourself most?

_____

_____

_____

Were you thinking of helping others?

_____

_____

_____

After making this review, do you need to ask for God's forgiveness?

_____

_____

_____

Reflection

Prayer

Lord, I pray to grow spirituality and work a long-term recovery program;

To daily examine myself;

To correct mistakes when I make them;

To take responsibility for my actions;

To be ever aware of my negative and self-defeating attitudes and behaviors;

To keep my self-will and need to control in check; and

To always remember I need your help;

Lord, keep me practicing humility and love toward others and continue in daily prayer in asking for your will to be done in my life as Lord and Savior.

STEP ELEVEN

I sought through prayer and meditation to improve
my conscious contact with God as I understood
Him, praying only for knowledge of His will and
the power to carry that out.

A healthy relationship requires communication and a willingness
to be yourself. If your spouse or companion chooses not to talk
honestly with you, your relationship will suffer in every area and may
eventually fail. When communication and honesty exist, relationships
are strengthened, and broken relationships can be healed. Your
relationship with God is your most important asset. Having a
relationship with God is impossible without communication. As
you draw nearer to God in prayer and meditation, you will draw
closer to peace and guidance.

As you continue to journey in the steps, you learn to recognize
problems, correct them properly, and continually seek God's
guidance. Spiritual growth within your personal transformation
occurs slowly—and only through discipline and reliance upon God.

Step Eleven is communicating with God. It is working through the practice of prayer and meditation. Through prayer, you talk to God and petition him. Through meditation, you listen to God and hope to hear his message for you. Step Eleven is about working to establish intimacy and learning the power of prayer and meditation. It is the act of drawing near to God and seeking his will for you.

Meditation is an important way of seeking God's will, of setting aside your own intentions, and of receiving God's guidance. When you combine prayer and meditation with self-examination, you discover the secret to successfully working the steps.

No matter how dedicated you are to recovery, you have moments of doubt about the direction of your life. Sometimes you might even question the need to continue working the steps. Sometimes you will be tempted to regress to your old compulsive behaviors. You will tend to feel weak when you feel pressured to succeed or when you expect events to follow your own schedule. In your frustration, you take control from God's hands and attempt to hasten the process through your own willfulness. When you do this, you are not following God's guidance and must renew the commitment you made in Step Three (surrendering your will and life to God).

Psalm 25:4–5 states, "Show me your way, Lord, teach me your path; guide me in your truth and teach me, for you are God my Savior, and my hope is in you all day long."

Step Eleven Study Guide

> Clean the slate, God, so we can start the day fresh!
> Keep me from stupid sins, from thinking I can
> take over your work; then I can start this day sun-
> washed, scrubbed clean of the grime of sin. These
> are the words in my mouth; these are what I chew
> on and pray. Accept them when I place them on the
> morning altar, O God, my Altar-Rock, God, and
> Priest-of-My-Altar. (Psalm 19:14)

> Show me how you work, God; school me in your
> ways. Take me by the hand; Lead me down the
> path of truth. You are my Savior, aren't you? (Psalm
> 25:4–5)

What has been your experience in prayer and meditation?

_____

_____

_____

_____

_____

_____

_____

_____

Cite a situation in which God showed you the correct path to follow. How did He reveal His will?

_____

_____

_____

_____

_____

_____

_____

_____

Describe a recent, stressful situation in which you took control away from God because of your doubts. Cite how God answered your prayers through another individual or a new experience.

_____

_____

_____

_____

_____

_____

_____

_____

List an area of your life where anxiety is a problem. Tell God about it in simple prayer. Write the prayer in the space below.

_____

_____

_____

_____

_____

_____

_____

_____

Describe how you are learning to hear God's voice. How is He speaking to you?

_____

_____

_____

_____

_____

_____

_____

_____

_____

_____

_____

_____

_____

Reflection

_____

_____

_____

_____

_____

_____

_____

_____

_____

_____

_____

_____

_____

_____

_____

_____

_____

_____

_____

_____

_____

_____

Prayer

Lord, I pray that you will always be first in my life and that I will keep my connection of trust with you open and clear from the confusion of my daily life. With prayer and meditation, I ask for freedom from self-will, my need to control, rationalization, and wishful thinking. I pray for Your gifts of honesty, open-mindedness, and positive action. Your will, Lord, not mine, be done.

STEP TWELVE

Having had a spiritual awakening as the result of
these steps, I tried to carry this message to alcoholics
and practiced these principles in all my affairs.

The twelve steps involve taking time to appreciate the spiritual
growth in your life. You work this step by sharing the program with
others and continuing to practice the principles of the steps in every
area of your life. You carry the message to those seeking recovery.
The more you help others, the more you will help yourself.

By sharing your own experiences and through prayer and meditation,
you are able to carry this message to those that are hurting and in
need of recovery. Telling your story will help others recognize their
need for a relationship with God and will encourage the growth of
your own humility.

Carrying the message gives you an opportunity to describe the ways in
which God's Spirit works through the twelve steps to transform your life.

Jewel Harper

Message

Each day your life experiences remind me of how you are renewed in your relationship with God. Through your sharing, you can convey the message of your experience, strength, and hope.

Step Twelve Study Guide

> Live creatively, friends. If someone falls into sin,
> forgivingly restore them, saving your critical
> comments for yourself. You might be needing
> forgiveness before the day's out. Stoop down and
> reach out to those who are oppressed. Share their
> burdens, and so complete Christ's law. If you think
> you are too good for that, you are badly deceived.
> (Galatians 6:1–2)

Discuss a recent situation in which you helped a newcomer. Describe your feelings. How did you encourage her or him?

_____

_____

_____

_____

_____

_____

_____

_____

What connection do you see between the twelve steps and Christianity?

_____

_____

_____

_____

_____

_____

_____

_____

Cite an example in which you realized that someone was behaving inappropriately and you were able to help that person take corrective action.

_____

_____

_____

_____

_____

_____

_____

_____

List a problem area in your life. Describe how you dealt with this problem by applying the twelve steps to it.

_____

_____

_____

_____

_____

_____

_____

_____

In what way is your new behavior positively influencing the lives of others?

_____

_____

_____

_____

_____

_____

_____

_____

Explain how your new behavior has frustrated people who knew you before your spiritual awakening.

_____

_____

_____

_____

_____

_____

_____

Share your story and spiritual awakening.

_____

_____

_____

_____

_____

_____

_____

Reflection

_____

_____

_____

_____

_____

_____

_____

_____

_____

_____

_____

_____

_____

_____

_____

_____

_____

_____

_____

_____

Prayer

Thank you, God, for each day becomes my new beginning. I am experiencing your miracles daily, and my spiritual awakening continues to unfold. I shall pass on the recovery tools that I have obtained to others, those that are hurting and in pain. For this opportunity, I am thankful. I pray with humility to continue walking day-by-day on the road of spiritual growth. I pray for inner strength and wisdom to practice the principles of this way of life in all I do and say. I need you, my family, friends, and the long-term recovery program every hour of every day.

MY MEMORY BOOK

Develop a memory book for yourself, and allow your memory book to cover an aspect of your life now that you are in recovery. Before you begin, take some quiet time to think about what you will focus on in your memory book. Allow God to take this journey with you. Make a list of people or things that are important in your life, talk with the people, and write stories about your experience with each person or thing. Gather pictures, mementos, and keepsakes; look for charms to represent the events you are writing about and put them together for a special treasure.

Because in long-term recovery each day becomes a new beginning for you, begin taking pictures or collecting them from family members and friends. Write the story about each memory on special paper next to your sobriety coins, photographs, and special treasure. Remember that treasures can be sobriety coins, pictures, music, poetry, and stories. If you are married or in a relationship, use current pictures as a couple. Include the story of your first encounter, dating years, and proposal. Write those stories and include them with your pictures.

Tell your story in your own words as if you were sharing the story with a friend.

No matter what type of memory book you are making, you can add another dimension by buying cards—speaking cards, musical cards, magazines that have spaces for photos, and holiday cards. Glue the speaking and music cards, magazines, newspapers, and holiday cards into the pages of your memory book, and bring their memories to life.

Reflection

_____

_____

_____

_____

_____

_____

_____

_____

_____

_____

_____

_____

_____

_____

_____

_____

_____

_____

_____

_____

_____

_____

_____

_____

Date: _____

Reflection

_____

_____

_____

_____

_____

_____

_____

_____

_____

_____

_____

_____

_____

_____

_____

_____

_____

_____

_____

_____

_____

_____

_____

Date: _____

Reflection

_____

_____

_____

_____

_____

_____

_____

_____

_____

_____

_____

_____

_____

_____

_____

_____

_____

_____

_____

_____

_____

_____

_____

Date: _____

Reflection

_____

_____

_____

_____

_____

_____

_____

_____

_____

_____

_____

_____

_____

_____

_____

_____

_____

_____

_____

_____

_____

_____

_____

Date: _____

Reflection

_____

_____

_____

_____

_____

_____

_____

_____

_____

_____

_____

_____

_____

_____

_____

_____

_____

_____

_____

_____

_____

_____

Date: _____

Reflection

_____

_____

_____

_____

_____

_____

_____

_____

_____

_____

_____

_____

_____

_____

_____

_____

_____

_____

_____

_____

_____

_____

_____

_____

Date: _____

Reflection

_____

_____

_____

_____

_____

_____

_____

_____

_____

_____

_____

_____

_____

_____

_____

_____

_____

_____

_____

_____

_____

_____

_____

_____

Date: _____

Printed in the United States
By Bookmasters